Tears Reap Joy

Restoration from the Inside Out

A Story of Forgiveness, Repentance

And Renewal

Written by

Tiffhany S. Bell

Purpose Publishing

1503 Main Street #168 ♨ Grandview, Missouri

www.purposepublishing.com

Copyright © 2017 Tiffhany S. Bell

ISBN: 978-0-997-98536-8

Editing by Felicia Murrell

Book Cover Design by PP Team of Designers

For permission and requests,

write to the publisher:

1503 Main Street, #168, Grandview, MO 64030.

Author Inquiries may be sent to tiffhanyspeaks@gmail.com

Those who sow in tears will reap with songs of joy.

-Psalm 126:5

Table of Contents

Prologue

The love of God is the beginning of wisdom, our promise to freedom and the truth to our future. As human beings, one of our greatest needs is to be loved. However, if there is any doubt that we are not loved, we will begin fostering sinful and dysfunctional behaviors to compensate for the distorted love that has fraudulently been exposed in our hearts. We will begin to search for things in other people, intrinsic elements that can only be fulfilled and then redeemed by God. We try to replenish a void with something people are incapable of providing. To know God is love, one must know that our sins have already been forgiven and in His love, we too, shall find the power of forgiveness. As love is the essence of God's being, forgiveness is essential for human survival. Forgiveness shows favor and it frees us from our past wrongs as well as takes away the power others may have over us. I had to learn that forgiving was not a feeling but an act followed by an emotion that is not easily obtained, nor easily given. For me, just hearing the word forgiveness conjured up many thoughts of hurtful experiences, but I knew I had to be transparent in my own transgressions. My past relationship with Christ was like a roller coaster ride. There were so many highs and lows, many times I was on fire for the Lord, while other times I was not so sure of His mercy.

As a result of my vague knowledge of God's favor, in those times of doubt and confusion I actually gave ground to the devil to enter into my life. The devil worked against me and through me. I was spiritually blinded. The devil quickly broke me down, just so he could slowly build me back up imposing as the broken spirit of virulence. The enemy latched on to my unforgiving heart, which then manifested into resentment. Before I knew it, the bitterness no longer colonized itself to one particular incident that had taken place. It had taken over every aspect of my life. Educating myself on the word of God not only allowed me to learn the true measure of forgiveness, it enabled me to become the woman I wanted my daughter to become and the woman I wanted my son to marry. There were many things in my life I was unable to see because my world became a pattern of destruction and dysfunctional bliss. With the renewing of my heart and thoughts, I had to break free from all positions leading to ungodly spiritual forces in the physical world that affected me in more than one way. The demons I came to know practiced many different methods to try and manipulate me, eventually these military like strategies were well planned out and used against me; internally, externally and through other people. I surrendered to the devil by birthing my survival through his sophisticated, relentless and provoked attacks. I was viable in my sin, giving a place in my heart for the devil to adversely disturb me, influence me and surround me with mayhem anyway he could. The spirits attacked my thoughts leading to my inability to be obedient to God's word. As I was in my heart, so I was in action.

God is a God of justice, turning my wrongs into rights. Many times, I did the right things with the wrong attitude and missed out on so many blessings. But with one touch of God's favor, He guided me to where I needed to be. Today, in Christ, I live and in my weakness I find His strength. The devil broke me to displace me, but God broke me for proliferation. Living as a true testament of God's favor, I first had to be broken before I was able to see myself honestly. I first had to die to live in the word of God. I needed to see myself to accept change starting with how I saw God. In the end, this would eventually determine how I changed. For many years, I lived my life seeing through the eyes of my own bitterness. When I lost my faith it caused me to lose sight of my path, ultimately, causing me to lose my truth. Through it all, I have learned that falling down is part of life but getting back up is part of living. Forgiveness brought me closer to God and I was able to not only have a stable relationship with Him but an intimate relationship as well. Forgiving also taught me that the people that hurt me in my past may have also had dealings with demons of their own. This allowed me to truly understand and come to terms with the fact that I had been dealing with ungodly spirits my entire life, operating in and rising up as the people I had grown to love. For they too inadvertently allowed the devil himself to become deep seeded in their hearts. The war I was fighting was not against a man or a woman, but against powers and principalities.

For we wrestle not against flesh and blood, but against princi-palities, against powers, against the rulers of the darkness of this world, against spiritual wickedness in high places (Ephesians 6:12).

For so long, the devil had permitted me to live in sin and at some point or another there had been an unspoken contract made between us to end my life. I knew my time living was nearing an end because there was always some type of affliction taking place. If I was not running for my life, I was pleading for it. At times I thought I had awakened from a bad dream just to find myself lying next to the devil himself. For I had known he would soon come reaping his wages of sin, my death. God promised me nothing would ever separate me from His love. He loved me despite my weaknesses, flaws and convictions. His love was not based on my performance or how long I walked in His faith. I got so wrapped up in doing something to make God love me more. I was begging for His favor, while demanding He do something for me, only willing to go so far for the Lord before I became transactional in my love for him. But because God has a unique love for me, I can only define His love as unconditional. Many times I forgot how far God's love could truly extend.

My heart would constantly remind me only God had the ability to take my sins and purify them. My greatest weakness turned into my greatest strength. The Bible taught me that true strength acknowledges weakness. God had a plan that was based on my faithfulness. This meant I not only had to forgive others, I had to also forgive myself and stop holding myself accountable for other people's mistakes. Subsequently, God used things I did not understand to push me into my purpose. I lost so many friends over the years. I could not comprehend why He was moving the wrong people out until I realized the relationship I was having with myself was a reflection of whom I allowed to enter into my life. So, I stopped hanging around myopic thinkers that lacked any discernment for their future because they could only offer me a short-range perspective on life.

I went through a season where I was hidden. In this time and in a very obscure manner, I was tested. I was frustrated and at my wits end with God, but I knew I had to show God my best even in the midst of all of my dis-ease with Him. What I did not understand was that if God was not able to trust me while I was hidden, He could not possibly trust me when it was time for me to be visible where the right people could find me, the right people could see me and the right people could celebrate me causing doors I thought would never open to be unlocked. God made a way for these Godly friendships to bloom, people that guided and mentored me every step of my journey. There was never any judgment, only honesty and security. Within those friendships, nothing was ever demanded of me. They made me a better person because they were living the best version of themselves. Before God sent His angels to work on my heart, I was driven by the lack of knowledge I had. But, through my obedience came breakthrough. In trusting Christ as my Savior, I was able to express my faithfulness through my actions. Embracing the act of forgiving allowed me to move forward by transforming the way I thought. The Lord had to teach me through revelation that we sow in one season and reap in another, but the devil was trying to get me to fall out of peace with an unforgiving spirit which would compromise my daily walk with God. Forgiveness allowed me to receive the healing I needed. Forgiving allowed me to surrender.

Chapter One

Seed of Rejection

I stare aimlessly at a photograph of my grandfather and I that stands untroubled at the top of my dresser, while somberly reflecting in tranquility as many unanswered questions intrude my mind. I recall the savory bread pudding my grandfather use to make. The notion soon evokes a sweet delightful aroma of cinnamon that casually entrenches my room. It jades my mood and swiftly triggers a trickle of bitter emotions that impedes upon my soul. I can feel his presence as I begin cursing him for all the pain he has caused, cursing him for the brokenness that weighs heavily on my soul. Immediately coming to the realization that my grandfather is the initial cause of my repulsive perceptions. He is the seed of my rejection, the eroding of my foundation of validity. He is the explanation of my depletion of self-assurance and the core cause of my doubt and instability to live freely in the perfect love I pursue, as I am conflicted with the imperfect love I give.

The root of my tattered love stems back to my childhood. Though I was well supported and cared for; even thought of as the golden child, the conflict started when I was very young. Growing up, I always craved love and attention and I knew my mother and uncles would provide me with whatever I wanted or needed. But the intent and interpretation of love was very different when it came to my grandfather. The intent was good coming from my uncles, but I could not interpret why my uncles loved me and my grandfather did not. How were my uncles able to show and express their love for me while I was left constantly bewildered as to why my grandfather never showed me the same type of love?

I have consumed my days longing for my grandfather's love. In return, my heart has been filled with unbearable pain. I've submerged myself in anguish, fearing that once I give my heart to a man, he too will eventually reject me just as my grandfather once did. Fearing the possibility of falling in love because a new romance would stimulate the induction of my past hurts. Unconsciously, I begin to shy away from love because this is when I am happiest, unguarded and vulnerable. Granting someone the opportunity to experience that part of me meant being as clever as the devil but twice as pretty. I was living with an infected soul unable to trust anyone. Suspicion became a compulsive reaction for me when the decision had not been made to forgive. And because of this, it was hard for me to treat people righteously. Consequently, in the end I would be unequal with love when it was time to render my feelings. A great deal of pain came as a result of living with a persistent, callous heart. In due time, my mind told my heart to stop evolving. I emotionally detached myself, ultimately leaving, because my fears were masked by many unjustifiable reasons for why things would never work out.

Internalizing many attitudes that I have held on to for far too long, acting as my own worst enemy with behaviors that slowly begin to industrialize my integrity, I soon began to hold back from my true passions in life and these behaviors start to form into self-sabotaging fears as I long for a fulfillment only God could provide. This was a source I depended on, not allowing Christ to enter into my heart to satisfy the thirst of my desires. This conventional way of thinking became a way of life for me. It was my normal. I invited the spirit of rejection to enter my heart and it settled. That is when I first welcomed the devil himself to have access to my heart. And because I was unable to forgive my grandfather for many years, I allowed myself to reap what I sowed. I was unable to sow mercy to my grandfather so I harbored anger that soon manifested into full blown bitterness. I sowed in judgment, failing to realize that when I chose not to forgive, I chose to be stuck in my past.

With every night that falls and every morning that arrives, I lay in bed quickly wiping the tears that slowly drop from my eyes. I allowed the sun to go down on my anger for many years allowing the devil to form a foothold of torture. Unpredictably, those same tears that fell from my eyes would someday help water my fields of joy. The tears were an invincible result of my irrational, distraught way of trying to make sense of my grandfather's status. Allowing myself to come to the conclusion that I was unlovable as my discerning innocence slowly destroyed my self-confidence. And because of this, I came up with a false believed perception of defeat that the color of darkness will forever be the warmth of my heart, the malice of life and the desire I solicit. The anguish I had restrained had finally won the battle over my rational philosophies and mental well-being. Sadly, I would continue to carry a heavy burden of bitterness most of my adult life.

For many years, I have struggled to come up with logical excuses for my grandfather, while trying to make a correlation between my happiness and a sense of satisfaction. Satisfaction solely acting as a sensational feeling that only provided me with what was desired for that moment of time and never replacing my emotional need for happiness. My flesh was greedy as satisfaction was my justification that kept me content and in need of wanting more, not realizing I was only satisfying the sin in me, slowly depriving myself of something that could only be experienced by a single gift of true friendship, joy. I was lusting for things that brought satisfaction to my desires for a short period of time; and once that satisfaction was fulfilled, I began to lust for something more because I was not in complete submission to God. And with real joy comes real pain. Satisfaction was my freedom. It was my way of keeping busy to avoid the loneliness. I thought I was healing from the pain, but I was still plagued by my grandfather's absence as I continued to feed my flesh with an unquenchable thirst.

I often forget people have lived life with struggles of their own, but I still wonder why my grandfather was so reluctant to try harder for a love that has since been terminated by the hands of time and for a questionable bond that has since been shattered by his rampant growth of demolished affection. Like a caged bird freed for the first time, I soon found myself wandering in my grandfather's endless blue summer sky, spreading my wings to meet the warmth of his distant rays of massive sunshine, anticipating that his radiance will brighten my days as a resolution for his absence. Why was my grandfather so uncommitted to his only grandchild, as he was duly committed to his many women and infinite flows of money? There are no tears that reap from joy, only isolation and solitude soon thereafter.

The first niece born from six uncles and one aunt, growing up I noticed the guilt that seeped from my uncle's eyes as they tried to mend my heart that would soon be broken and weakened by my grandfather. Protectors of my divine will as a result of my grandfather's failure for not being an active father in their lives. My protectors, protecting their 'only child' for one simple purpose, they knew one day he would inflict the same pain in my life as he once did in theirs. And because of this guilt, my uncles learned to embrace. Out of duty and obligation, they stepped up and took my grandfather's place.

My grandfather was a mystery to me, as it has been over twenty years since his passing. I do not remember much about him, not even the sound of his voice, only the darkness of his skin and his towering slender frame. For indescribable reasons, I have kept his spirit alive all these years for my selfish yearning of his endless conversation, wisdom, and thrills from the stories my grandfather use to tell. I have welcomed his presence with my daunting efforts in dedication to him in all that I do; an indissoluble soul tie that keeps me in bondage. I know it is my granddad that whispers softly in my ear as I lay comfortably asleep at night, awakened by the wind of his breath that quickly sweeps the hairs on the back of my neck as the faint sugary aroma of cinnamon calmly fills the air. I know it is him that raises his voice so forcefully it causes me to awaken from my sleep confused in fear. In the uncertainty, I yell out to my son in the middle of the night thinking it is his voice coming from his room. I soon realize he is fast asleep, as I stand bewildered in the doorway of his room. I turn to the light that dimly shines from the bathroom entrance and quietly whisper, "Granddad?" With no response, I call to him once more. This time much louder as I weep in grief, frightfully hoping to hear the sound of his voice once more. I stand consciously aware, frightened from the possibility that he may answer me. I stand patiently waiting. Is it my grandad I hear when I get so anxious and worked up? Is it my grandad I hear when I begin to stress about life's oppressions that are not controlled by my fate? Is it you, Granddad, the protector of my home, the protector of my worry, the protector of my unforgiving brokenness?

Sorrowed by the notion that we will never have the opportunity to spend more time together, exhausted from pondering the possibilities of endless memories we could have shared and weakened by the thought of not having him by my side for every accomplishment, victory, heartbreak, or for the births of his beautiful great-grandchildren. To this day, no one ever talks about my grandfather. Whenever his name is spoken, I can see the hurt on everyone's face as their body language starts to change, a sense of uneasiness fills the room. Incapable of justifying why I still need him after all these years, I try to conceal the love I have for him out of fear that no one will ever understand why I feel this way. My secret love that lingers for him remains disguised; as he is known to be the unspoken disease that continues to dwell on in so many broken, angered hearts.

Deeply submerged in anguish, desperately in need of gratification for why he left me to fill a void that will never be filled, I continue to live my life on an endless search for his existence. In search of something I will never be able to feel nor see, I continue striving for moments in time looking for an attachment that I will never be able to experience. And no matter what I do or how hard I contend, there will always be an emptiness that resides deep within. Unable to rest because I am striving for his love and replacing it with perfection and revulsion, I understand my feelings of emptiness is not a trait of genetic inheritance but something I have made a concrete aspect for so many years of my life and because of this, nothing will ever be good enough for me, just average.

My grandfather was a worldly man, a well-known fornicator whose disenchanted lifestyle ultimately took his life. The time to pay his wages to sin was due. My grandfather was an entrepreneur, a pimp by night and by day he operated his own cab service. Taken from us before it was his time, his death came as a sudden tragic shock. I wished I could have shed a tear at his funeral, but I was too young to understand. Now, as time goes on, I am currently making up for that lost day, detaining myself at times from loving. Not fully understanding what his passing meant back then and how it would impact my life in the present, I have always had this overwhelming sense of failure growing up. At times I often found myself making constant comparisons with other girls that had loving grandfathers in their lives. Learning how to overcome this feeling has been one of my greatest challenges thus far. Quickly absorbing what the true definition of resilient really meant fueled me with a desire to find it in myself. I soon realized it is never too late to love. However, not knowing exactly how to open my heart to receive it has been a very difficult task to execute. It has taken me some time to acknowledge that my grandfather's failure to form a healthy relationship with me was my strength to flourish into a beautiful cold hearted woman with a tainted heart and to love no one that ever showered me with loyalty or affection because that was their sign of vulnerability. For so long, I have coped with the truths from his past wishing they were all fictitious. Yet, I still managed to blame myself for my grandfather not wanting to be a part of my life. I now realize that he was the one who missed out and it was not me who failed, but a man that I still cherish to this day who was incapable of showing his devotion to his grandchild.

Forever will I treasure the small portion of memories I have of him. He grew as I grew, never fading with time. My grandfather was a temporary warmth that hastily tore me apart. I kept him alive, battling with the pain, which supplied me the ambition to celebrate his life, even in his death. I have been living my life entirely dependent on the strength of my longing for his existence, now knowing the only way I will be able to live life and be happy in it is if I let the thought of my granddad go and allow him to rest after all these years. The worst part of holding on to his memory was not the pain I felt or the loneliness that came with it but my fiendish personality that was created because of it. My grandfather will always be a part of me but keeping him alive was causing me to lose my way in life. I am walking around abandoned from the world and isolated from the chance of letting true love in to help mend what he once shattered, my heart.

I resisted forgiving my grandfather because at the time I really did not understand how forgiveness worked. I was unfairly suffering from my grandfather's actions. Forgiveness for me was a decision to let go. I was so wrapped up in all the wrong my grandfather did I was unable to see my present happiness. I brought bitterness into every relationship and new experience I had. Because of my bitterness, I lost very valuable and quite possibly, enriching connections with others. I had to move forward and away from the "victim" role by releasing the power my grandfather had over me. I no longer allowed this control to define my life, filling my heart with so many vain and empty things. I found compassion through the restoration of my heart. From my love of God, I received the wholeness I longed for. The Lord came to me, reigning peace and an inner strength filled with new hope.

I am releasing my grandad from my mind, as I will always keep the memories from the photograph of us close to my heart, permanently relieving myself from this self-inflicted anguish and replacing it with being content in knowing that what is done is done. I am learning how to move forward by giving myself an opportunity to discover who I truly am without him. And with a matured heart, I am now able to affirm my undying love that grows each and every day for him. With no regards for what anyone else may think or feel, for the first time since I was a little girl, I am able to speak the very same words that caused me so much heartache and pain, finally ready to let go and set his spirit free.

Rest in peace, James Franklin Copper, I love you dearly.

This next chapter is dedicated to all the girls whose father broke their hearts before any boy could.

Chapter Two

My Bondage to Sin

Growing up, I spent a lot of time surrounded by the love of my uncles. My mother, my grandmother and four of my uncles shared the same last name. I remember questioning my mother often about the difference in my last name. My youngest uncle always teased me about having a different name from the rest of my family, jokingly telling me I was adopted. Any chance my uncle would get, he reminded me I was adopted. I would then question my mom. The first few times, my mother explained she gave me my father's last name just as they all shared my grandfather's last name. It made sense to me. I knew it was true. But deep inside, I innocently wished it wasn't. I wanted to be adopted. Maybe if I were adopted, it would not hurt as much knowing my father rejected me. The thought of being adopted brought a sense of relief, but it also plagued my thoughts leaving an unsettled cogent reason for his rejection of me. I desperately wished I was not his. This was my only justification and the only reason that made sense as to why I was not loved by my father.

I did not have the typical father/daughter relationship with my father. We did not share any hugs or I love you's. Although we shared the same last name, I was his burden. I was brought into this world blemished with blame. I lacked the knowledge of what a healthy relationship should be like between a man and a woman. I never knew the importance of having a positive relationship with my dad and how this could influence my standards and choices. This lead to repeated dysfunctional relationship decisions. I often settled, constantly wondering why I always ended up with the same type of men. It was because I was searching for and trying to fix my father. This was my affliction, a reflection of not trusting and honoring the strong black man. I would degrade and disrespect them, projecting on to them how I felt about my father my entire life. Untrustworthy, neglectful man that he was, and now I have inflicted those same thoughts on all black men.

There I stood incapable of loving a man because my father was incapable of loving me. Left too weak to believe in love, I became a slave to my own bondage. For most of my life, I lived being spiritually restrained. I was unable to prevail in my purpose because I had been held captive to my own sin. I was a subject to my own oppression forming chains that only my Savior could break. I harbored anger in my heart that started off innocently then took the form of unforgiving assumptions, which quickly turned into resentment, which then manifested into retaliation. Unable to regain control of my emotions, I quickly became stirred up with a multitude of sullen behaviors from an impression that was embedded in me since childhood. The act of retaliation helped feed the anger eventually turning into full-blown bitterness. Seeing that my grandfather and my father were equally accountable, I saw everything through the eyes of bitterness. I fault them both. Their rejection caused me to flourish as a heartless young girl. It was the love I needed from my father most of all. The rejection from my daddy molded me into a heartless woman leaving me with little faith and confidence in understanding the dynamics of the males' role and their position in the home. Now, I effortlessly walk away at the first sign of trouble in all my relationships, platonic and romantic. This was my victory, my pleasure seeing others hurt, as I was sinfully bitter. I knew this was not right. I looked in the mirror and saw a clear reflection of my father. I had given my father control over my life, even in his death, by allowing him to inflict his harsh ways into my thoughts. His unacceptable way of life and my hurting was the only way I could live.

And because this became a way of life for me, when someone hurt me, I would lust for them harder. I needed to fix them. I gave many people many chances to continuously hurt me. The more chances I gave someone, the less respect they had for me. The more chances I gave, the more they showed me how unafraid they were of losing me. For they knew that no matter what they did, I would refuse to walk away from them, and I also knew in my heart no matter what they did I would not walk away from them. Because there had been an ungodly soul tie that was formed, an unseen power of control the devil had placed before me pulled me from my place of peace. Being around other broken, dysfunctional people made me feel better. I thought two broken people together would become whole by building what little strength we had on each other and mending each other's brokenness. Instead, my strength should have come from God. I thought if I borrowed some of their strength, it would increase my faith when it came to forgiving my father. There was never any redemption for my actions.

My dad was supposed to be my first true love, the first real man to not only teach me but also show me what unconditional love meant and how unconditional love was supposed to feel. Looking to him as my knight in shining armor anticipating his weaponry to keep me unscathed from the harsh realities and perfidies of the world, I quickly became fully cognizant that there was always an underlying deficiency between us, devoid of many realistic illustrations of how a healthy father/daughter relationship was expected to be. My father's lessons in life were nothing more than false hope and wishful thinking that one day his feelings for me would change. Through the guidance that only a father can give his little girl, he was supposed to teach me that being vulnerable is only half the battle and that falling in love involves a lot of risks. He was supposed to encourage me to be a risk taker. My father was supposed to show me by his actions that there is absolutely nothing wrong with being vulnerable and defenseless in front of the one person your heart belongs to. My daddy never showed me that if I build the faith to trust the person I love as God, then my heart would never be broken. Instead, my father taught me to live my life afraid to fall in love and not to trust or expose my vulnerability to anyone. Just being around real love and a team that genuinely loved one another would annoy me. I would stray away from people that knew real love. I thought they would see right through my brokenness and unmask my insecurities. Seeing happy people was a constant reminder of everything I so desperately wanted. And at some point, I knew I had become addicted to dysfunctional brokenness. So I continued to surround myself with toxic relationships because the devil made it perfectly clear that I was not good enough to experience being loved.

My father was supposed to teach me that perfection is a myth. This probably explains my striving for perfection. Now my emotional decisions are governed by the time I spend trying to suppress my perfectionistic ways better known as obsessive compulsions. And because I have accepted the spirit of rejection, I am an over achieving perfectionist because nothing in my eyes will ever be good enough. I was never good enough for my father, so I will never be good enough for anyone or anything. Is my life so orderly because I felt displaced my entire life? Naively, my father exceedingly deposited disorder in my life.

Still a boy not yet a man, unskilled at life, he set out to find adventure, quick thrills, and unforgettable pleasures. Reluctant to change, my father could have ended the cycle of disparity and fostered a good life for us. I have held him accountable for my displacement in this world and for my inability to love and trust another human being, which left me with a strong uncertainty of the black man's role in many of my relationships. His life lessons were supposed to be teachable moments that stuck with me throughout life, demonstrating a true act of kindness by unselfishly leaving his legacy of hope behind. My father never showed me that a man would sail to the end of the earth to get to me if he really wanted to. I can never recall a single time that my father attended a birthday, a graduation or called just because.

Over and over, I paint this colorful fairytale image of my father saving the day and looking to him as my hero. I have painted an image that portrays him to be this strong, affectionate, devoted, wise man, mastering his manner as I sit in awe using my father as an example replicating his way of life, failing to realize this fairytale image of him I created was my colorless, distorted reality. Using his techniques of abandonment by abandoning many that have not only proved their love for me but also displayed their loyalty and because I mastered this characteristic of his, I am unable to give love purely because my father tainted me with a vision that my heart is unable to let go. Sadly, abandonment has become a way of life for me. Attaching myself to weak, neglectful, dishonest, foolish boys not yet men turned men. My father never warned me that bad boys are fun, but there is no changing them and to never seriously date a man I would never consider marrying. I preferred the "bad boy" type because they were everything I looked for in my father. A quick thrill of excitement and unreserved with their affection. In my late teens, when I was able to date, I took a strong interest in "bad boys." Most of the guys I dated were either drug dealers, well known to the streets, or had a bad reputation. These guys were mysterious to me. They were everything I was not. They were nothing I knew about my grandfather and everything I knew of my father and his mysterious life. That was just the type of excitement I sought.

Out of my own desperation, I settled for what I thought I was good enough for. Only using prayer to pray for what I wanted instead of praying for God's plans for me in terms of a man. I now know the true meaning of, "Be careful what you pray for, because you may actually get it."

I have lived my life evolving into my father, as I am emotionally unavailable and unable to love with a clean, clear heart. Assuming anyone who ever opens their mouth to declare their love for me are only out to hurt me and will eventually have some sort of ulterior motive to break my heart. His love for me was forsaken. My father left me alone and because of this I still struggle to figure out what it is everyone sees in me and exactly what it is they love about me since my father was unable to communicate his love to me. Destroyed by my very own perception of who I am, not fully able to comprehend nor control how I respond to pain, I naively engage in hurtful tactics to those that show me the slightest bit of love, utilizing the clever characteristics of desertion I learned from my father. I prey on the flaws of others using it to my advantage. "Leave them before they leave me," was a motto I lived by, yet I managed to be envious of the possibility to love and be loved, not ever giving anyone a chance to get too close to me, only allowing them a restricted amount of time in my life before making up some lame excuse for why I no longer needed them. There were never any explanations, phone calls, or forms of closure, just the changing of my phone number. I realized this was not me fleeing from the possibilities of love or excusing people out of my life; it was God preparing and leading me in my purpose. I made others feel rejected with a strong sense of abandonment. Sadly, that was all I knew. Welcome to my colorless, distorted way of life. But maybe I needed to be broken and placed in dysfunctional relationships so I could learn how to appreciate a good man once he crossed my path. Maybe God had something great planned for me even when it felt like I was taking a loss in many of my relationships. But in the same breath, I was asking God to send me a whole man. A God-fearing Christian man so he could love me back to right as I was this broken woman only willing to love half-heartedly. Now, I understand God created woman so the man could see himself in her. The woman is supposed to be the splitting image of the man, his backbone and his helpmate. A helpmate suitable just for him. I had the wrong attitude, my attitude was, "What can you do for me, instead of how can we help each other."

My father's negligence to apologize or offer any explanation for why he was never involved as a father has affected me negatively causing me to become vindictive. I have always longed to be daddy's little girl. I never needed monetary gifts or sympathy. I just needed to be showered with love and affection. I just needed my daddy. At no time in the past, or my future, will I ever know what it feels like to be daddy's little girl. Instead, I am left with an inability to forgive, building walls to protect myself, walls that exist solely to see if anyone will ever have the strength to knock them down. What I didn't learn from my father is that the secret to happiness is acceptance of myself and in order for me to find acceptance I would have to be willing to make a decision to forgive. I would have to start knocking down my own walls, which seemed like an impossible feat to me.

I have been predisposed with a mixed blessing. A blessing that has both the advantage and disadvantage of discovering someone's weakness as I learn by observing their ways and eventually using their weakness to my benefit. Having this sort of mixed blessing requires one to be heartless and have the capability to become insensible in any given situation. It requires someone to be powerless in their own feelings so they are unable to empathize with the feelings of others. This type of affliction settles only in a broken and infuriated heart. It emerges over time and once it has taken form, there is no stopping its fury. For I allowed the spirit of anger to attach itself to me and become deep seated. Known to many as my alter ego, a goddess acting as the defender of moral order, represented by true darkness. For I am her. I am the agony that greets you with a vengeful mind and a rage that welcomes you with an inviting body of thought. For I have turned my vengeful fury against those that are wholesomely innocent. As a consequence, they too shall stand in the path of my wrath. They too shall be punished by affiliation. Weakened by the thought of love, I begin to find strength from the emotional pain I caused others. I have allowed the spirits of discouragement and resentment to rise and take their positions in my life.

As my relationship grew stronger with God, He told me to take a look at myself. I knew if I really wanted to be delivered and live with a clean heart, I had to stop playing the victim in my failed relationships. I had to take responsibility and say it was something in me. And, since I was in sin, it was something in my flesh that attracted me to these men and many of my friendships. The only thing we had in common was brokenness, lust and mystery. Relationships wholly established by the enemy that stemmed from an extended branch of untold truths. Everyone was to blame except me. It was easy for me to pass judgment and not deal with my issues. I walked around with a lustful, scorned heart, and ultimately that is what I attracted. I was not able to grow until I was able to identify and repent. It all started to make sense to me. I was dealing with people who themselves had ungodly spirits attached to them, which was why it was so hard for me to break away from the pain and hurt. I was soul tied with these broken, worldly relationships. A lot of people do not know they are bound by these spirits, and I did not recognize what I was dealing with because I was in sin myself.

A father's love is secured by his own self-reflection and where he is in life. His experiences in life are the sole reflection of all that he has loved, lost and experienced and as a failed result of this I lived a lie. I was living my life pretending. I was living my life based on what other people had. Over the years, I searched for things that would make me happy, things that would help fill my father's void. Many times I was so frustrated with God. I was impatient and never allowed God to extend His grace in my life. I limited my blessings from God because I centered my life on everyone else's life and what they had. Their success had to be my success and should have been my success because I deserved it. I was distracted and never at peace with myself because I was constantly comparing myself to that of what others had.

My father was a mystery to me. My memories of him as a child are vague. I only heard one consistent story leading to my father's return home and I depended on that one story. That one story helped my mind form an idea about the type of men I would find intriguing. See, my father and I had a bit of a relationship when I was too young to remember until one day he decided to leave and move out of state. It would be years, before I saw him again...seventh grade exactly.

That year, my mother came to me with a serious look in her eyes and told me she had received a phone call. My father had returned home and my mother wanted to know if I wanted to see him. To me, seeing my father was not a big deal. I had so many questions I wanted to ask, and I wanted to see what he looked like because it had been so long since I had seen his face that I could not remember what he looked like. I could not remember the sound of his voice, the color of his eyes or how tall he was. All these thoughts and emotions hit me at once. There was no need to think about it or try to figure anything out. I had to see my dad. I responded to my mother with a resounding "yes!" My mother told me my dad was in the hospital. She wanted me to know before she made the arrangements for me to see him. My father had been shot and was paralyzed from the neck down. I think I might have faded away for a second trying to take this in because my mom kept asking me if I heard what she said. All the thoughts I had soon turned into fear, fear of how I would react seeing a man that I spent countless nights wondering if he was thinking about me. Fear that I would not be so welcoming at his return home. Fear because I knew the only reason he returned home was not because of me but because he was left with no other choice.

Disappointment filled my heart, but I still loved him. I still needed to see him, and a part of me wanted to know what happened to him and why he was paralyzed. My mother did not say much afterward in regards to my dad. She just made the arrangements for me to see him. A few days passed and soon we were on our way to the hospital. Nothing I had ever experienced could compare to the joy I felt in my heart that day. My spirit was free and for the first time in a long time. I would no longer feel misunderstood. I would no longer feel rejected but accepted by my father because I knew that when I saw my dad, all my broken pieces would finally fit together and I would be whole again.

We arrived at the hospital. The only way I could remain calm as my mother and I walked the halls was to play out how I thought things would be, not realizing I had fantasized a grand reunion. I imagined my father running to me and giving me this big bear hug, reluctant to let me go. I was confident approaching the door to the room. I had completely forgotten my father was paralyzed and became so overjoyed with these thoughts, I quickly opened the door to his room expecting a warm welcome and there he lay, comfortably snuggled in his bundle of blankets. My heart dropped and suddenly these fears circled my thoughts. I looked to my mother for comfort. She gave me a nod and I entered his room. There was no warmth from a hug upon my arrival, only stillness and a big courageous smile. Finally, the moment of truth, there I was staring at my reflection in his face. There he lay, the man I hated to love. The man that left me because I was not good enough to love. In that moment, the built up anger I had softened just a bit. Seeing my dad like that did something to me. I let my guard down. I allowed myself to be defenseless. I was vulnerable in the light of his smile. That was something I had not done in long time. I exposed my love for him in that small room and he felt it. On that day, my love was all he needed. I never got around to asking him what happened. I never got around to indicting him for why he was never there for me. But that day, because the hands of time stopped, to him I was his little girl and that was all that mattered.

The moment I saw my father, I realized people really do love us. They just don't know how to love us. I realized, in all those years leading up to that moment, I loved my father even through the pain of his unknown presence. I just did not know how to love him. Because he was not in my life, I had no way of loving him. It was kind of like out of sight out of mind type of love. God had to work on my father and even though it was in a bad way, He brought my father back to me so I could show him what love really was. I forgave my father that day with the thought that maybe love was void in his life preventing him from fully knowing how to love me. Maybe someone he loved did not love him, causing a void in his heart, consciously projecting that void onto me. Maybe that was his definition of love. Maybe he thought because he loved me, I would be better off without him. Maybe he was not being selfish at all.

My memory of my dad was nothing more than a deteriorated figment of my imagination, a thought I had given too much power. My emotional reaction has been justified and the only real image I now have of my father is that of my brother. My father passed years later due to infection. My son was three at the time. My father never revealed to me what really happened before he came back home. I lost my father but gained a sister, meeting her for the first time at my father's funeral. I had finally built a relationship with my dad. The hardest thing I had to deal with in his passing was not saying goodbye, it was learning how to live without him again and the emptiness from knowing in spirit there could never be another substitution for his presence.

Chapter Three

Anticipated Deception

*B*eautifully imperfect, I knew I loved you long before I ever saw you. You are the strength that keeps my heart anchored. You are my rock, my everlasting joy. Born in the eleventh month of the year, spiritually, you are my revelation and face of true love. Beautiful, silky, alluring toffee complexion, ravishing personality, your calm spirit is a true representation of who you are. Your beautiful hazel eyes have revealed to me many stories over the years. When God created you, He gave me something to fight for. That something was love.

It was my son's choice to come through my body. I truly believe he has been here before. We are all souls born into a different body. Maybe my son was my father and I was his daughter in a different life creating this connection of energy between us. In life before birth, my child chose me. He saw the pain in my eyes before he was even born. He knew I needed him. He knew his existence would change my life. Believing my son chose me as his mother teaches me the meaning of unconditional love. He arrived here with everything he needed to know about me with the clear purpose to make me love again. My son is my greatest spiritual teacher. Because of him, I understand that I chose my parents, which is why forgiving my father was so important to me. My son taught me that he will break my heart, but in the end, I will still love him and as his mother I would break his heart, but in the end he still loves me. I know in life this cannot be helped and part of growing up for me was learning to forgive my father for any hurt he caused me. How could I hold any bitterness or resentment towards my father when the hurt he caused me was ultimately what I chose for him to do? I chose my parents because they were the lessons I needed to learn. My son chose me because I am a lesson he needs to learn.

And as I look at my son, unable to distinguish manhood and leaving the nest from deception, I fear in my reality, here my son is another man that will too soon reject me. Unable to distinguish this reality that every man I have ever loved has failed me by leaving me from the nature of adulthood. Anticipating this deception, my brokenness leaves me yet again consumed by the spirit of rejection. Often times when we have been broken for so long, we become selfish not only in the flesh but in our thinking, causing this spirit to enter our soul and take over our mind. This spirit's objective is to hinder. Rejection is my bondage to sin. Too afraid to tell my only son "I love you" in fear he will walk out.

Finding myself yelling at my son in frustration for his unkempt room. Frustration turned into annoyance, and then I became infuriated. This anger stemmed from something I had been holding back for many years. This aggravation was no longer controlled by frustration from an unkempt room. It was fueled by years of rejection, and everything I ever wanted to say to my father seeped from the lips of my mouth onto my child. It was no longer about a dirty room. I open fire on my son with my angry words because in my eyes, I would push him away like I pushed every other man out my life. Maybe I could push him into rejecting me because I knew he loved me with all that he was. Loving my son meant chastising him for my father's mistakes. The deception I knew I would be unable to control once my son reached a certain age and wanted to explore his manhood. The deception I had talked with my son about many times in preparation for his college years outside our home state of Kansas. The fact that I had sat down with my son many times and advised him that in order to really become a man he needed to leave the nest and explore life away from home, explaining that choosing a college away from home would allow him to figure out who he was. This was the anticipated pain I inflicted upon myself. I would be unable to distinguish his manhood from yet another man leaving me.

My bond with my daughter is unbreakable. I make it a priority to hug and kiss her daily. But I have to work to hug and kiss my only son. I know it has a lot to do with my past relationships with men and my emotionally distant father, but I am so afraid that if I inundate my son with affection, he too will walk out on me. But I still love my son with all my heart. He is the only reason I hold on to the little hope that there are good men in this world. My son has broadened my horizon on so many aspects of my life. He completes me. He makes me whole.

As a mother, the bond of love I share with my son is one of the most enduring experiences life has to offer, but also one of the hardest things to break when it is time for my son to leave. I know I will soon be confronted with the reality of letting go of the only man that stuck around for the past thirteen years; just long enough to love me through all my flaws while never passing judgment. In my heart, once he turns eighteen, I will always have this void that I did not give my son enough love. Could I ever give him enough love? Or am I dependent on the love my son has for me?

My son has opened my heart as I nurtured him, provided for him and loved him unconditionally. The day is fast approaching for me to welcome him to the world. My son has provided me the strength I needed and when he leaves the nest, a piece of that strength will leave with him. I know God has given my son responsibilities and one day he will need to become the man God intended him to be. Soon my son will leave and stand independently of me. In letting him go, I will lose my self-identity. Seeing nothing but his face through my struggles, he has kept me grounded. I will never have my son as a child again, losing the warmth of his love, quickly finding my heart under pressure, creating a sense of loss, as I anticipate his deception.

With each passing year, my son has given me a new perspective about men. I have learned to appreciate the male role, which was foreign to me. My son has taught and proven to me that not all men are the same. He has taught me self-worth through his unconditional love for me, treating me with nothing but utmost respect.

Today, I am to my children who my father was unable to be to me, an opportunity of love. I had to be this perfect woman to my children. I had to be this way because I did not want my children to grow up and experience any pain. I did not realize that I was trying to give my children everything my grandfather and father did not give me. And when I look at my children, I see the best of me. They are all the things that are good in me. They are the love I once lost.

I started to question my behavior. I felt like I had all this love to give but no one to share it with. I was too afraid to trust emotionally and began to channel all my love into my children, sheltering them from the harmful realities of my past. Is there such a thing as loving your children with all of your heart as a form of protection because I never wanted my children to ever feel rejected and experience the pain I once did? I love my children with my whole heart, but I was only giving a friendship/relationship half-hearted truths.

> To my handsome son
> I love you for all that you are,
> all that you have been and all that you are yet to be.
> My beautiful daughter, you are my gift from heaven.

Chapter Four

Married to Sin

*I*t took me many different seasons to understand what God was doing to prepare me for what He had in store. It also took me some time to realize the reason why I was being attacked. I was in love with the thought of being in love and in return, I lusted from the thought perceiving it to be love. Not only did the devil see this in me, he also saw something great and did not want me to move forward in my destiny. He would condemn me and because I was still bitter in my heart, I allowed the devil to use me. But God's glory and unconditional love saved me, and my alter ego that started at birth ended in death through my repentance.

Because I was rejected as a child, I acted out as an adult, demanding the attention I failed to receive from the men I loved. Turning twenty-one was a rites of passage for me. I sought attention by fostering sinful behaviors. Anyone who knows me, knows I am a shy, reserved and very conservative person. But, my rejection led to an alter ego and by nightfall, I was a completely different person. Turning twenty-one allowed me to live again. I was able to do and say things I was unable to do being the shy, reserved girl everyone knew. Partying four days a week, Thursday night into Monday morning with little sleep in between and sipping on the devil's juice became huge priorities in my life. I still held down my job, paid my bills and took care of my son. I had a mentality that helped sustained me in my present condition which was a stronghold the devil used against me.

My alter ego Diva exuded fabulous style, rocking nothing but the best. I would get all dressed up with flashy revealing clothing and jewelry. My toes and nails stayed done. I had to have things my way or no way at all. No one stood in my way. This character of mine made me stand out in a way that regular old Tiff would never have the guts to do. I became self-absorbed. Every night before I went out, I blasted music in my house while getting ready. This became a ritual for me, as music is a conjuring for demons because demons are attracted to chatter. I was idolizing things I had no clue about, chanting many songs that glorified the word diva. With the music blasting, I chanted lyrics at the top of my lungs conjuring up her spirit. Diva is actually, Deva an ancient Buddhist goddess sent from Satan. This Deva spirit would arise in me. Calling her name allowed me to manifest her goddess spirit. People worshiped her beauty, earrings and clothing. I became her. I was this goddess in the flesh as I served two gods. I no longer felt rejected. Men could not resist me as I put on the image of the devil himself, because the devil's only objective is to take authority from men and use seduction to destroy them. I was as clever as the devil but twice as pretty.

And with a beautifully tainted heart, lust was an unexplained action that made me irrational in my thoughts, often times mistaking lustful feeling for those of a predestined soul mate. My lustful feelings were a superficial surface of my ignorance. I learned that I had an aura within me that only ungodly men could sense. I was a worldly woman. Therefore, worldly men approached me. I never understood this philosophy. Worldly men looked at me through the eyes of their flesh. Worldly men asked me out because they found me physically attractive. My physical attributes were what society considered beautiful. Worldly men are power-seekers led by their flesh and culture. Their attention to women is vain. A man of God looks at women through the eyes of Christ. Yes, looks may matter, but a man of God is mostly attracted to a woman's unfading beauty of her inner self. A man of God does not need the validation of a woman because God has already validated his thoughts. Just because someone calls themselves a Christian does not mean they are holy. Too often, I fell for people and befriended them because they were religious. I quickly found out that just because someone called themselves a Christian did not mean they were spiritual. In this world, there are three types of people.

The first is the "religious person," then there is the "spiritual person" and last, the "holy person." There is a valid distinction between the three. I mainly associated with religious individuals because I myself was religious. I was still young to the word of God. I was a Christian that picked out a few things I wanted to do right in my life. Religion is a set of beliefs formed in an institution of organized structure. This sort of structure removes God from the equation. I went to church to worship. I was told what to pray, told what to believe and study. Church was the place I was supposed to go to confess all my sins to a member of clergy versus going directly to God himself and confessing my sins, all of which removed me from God.

A *religious person* feeds off the fruit of a poisonous tree. They believe in God but are attracted to carnal things. Religion is often forced, only calling on God in a time of need. There is not an intimate relationship. Christ was only relied on to fulfill a need or want. A religious person has not submitted themselves to God. They still gamble, party and curse, etc. They see nothing wrong with committing adultery. Religious people often worship idols such as singers, rappers, actors and actresses. Religion is placing faith in the tangible aspects of life. With religious people, there is one simple moral code, to do as you please during the week, and then dedicate one day for going to church on Sunday, listen to the message and as soon as you leave the church parking lot, return to your old ways. Religious people are moved by what others are doing, what culture and society says is in, and desires to please oneself more than God. Religious people know the word of God and can quote a few scriptures, but may not understand the word in its entirety. I was religious in my ways.

A *spiritual person* can be defined as one that is in the process of personal transformation and psychological growth. Spirituality is born in a person and is developed in a person's mind, body and soul. This is where I am at currently in my life. My spirituality was born through my revelation. A spiritual person has a much more elevated knowledge of God's will than the religious person. A spiritual person seeks guidance from God before making any move or decision. A spiritual person is born out of their spirituality. People seek and choose to be spiritual. I learned that spirituality is something that cannot be found in a church.

Religion is based on rituals and formality and requires guidance from others. Things are taught that may not be in the Bible whereas spirituality is taught through self-discipline and obedience. Religiousness does not investigate nor does it question. It lives in your thoughts whereas spirituality gives you inner peace. There is not one religion but hundreds, whereas spirituality is infinite. Religiousness questions and lives in your conscience. Religion seeks you, whereas spirituality causes you to seek.

Then there is the *holy person* that is known by their fruit and not by their church attendance. They live a life of holiness through their total devotion to God. Holiness is wholeness. To be holy is to be distinct, living by God's specific standards so the world can know you belong to God. As a believer, you should be set apart from the world living by God's standards not societies. God is not calling holiness to be perfect but to be distinct from the world and to not be afraid to live out your distinctiveness in your day-to-day life. True believers recognize their position in Christ while allowing the Holy Spirit to be their source of power and guidance. They are absent of greed, jealousy, pride, anger, slander, hatred, and attachment.

I bounced from one unhappy relationship to another, entering into relationships for the wrong reasons, trying to fix my brokenness. I was dependent upon the love and fulfilment I was desperately seeking. I never allowed myself to heal. I never allowed myself to figure out who I was as an individual or, most importantly, who I was as a woman. Sadly, there was never any time spent in reflection. If I had, I could have built a relationship based on the strength of God instead of attracting men that were the spitting image of my flesh. I learned in my transformation that a worldly man plays on a woman's challenges from her past. A man of God quickly takes notice of a woman's perplexities, confusion and distress and instead of using her flaws against her; he welcomes them with unconditional zeal.

Often times, I found myself lying next to the devil himself. My bed became the altar as I indulged in sinful behaviors, illegally marrying every man I slept with. It was not because I was unpracticed in the will of God. I knew what I was doing was wrong. I was doing it because I thought I was hurting God since he allowed so many to hurt me. I was in a state of rebellion. God intended sex to be between a husband and his wife, not whomever I chose to have it with. The intentions for sex between a husband and his wife is to form a soul tie that keeps them together through sickness and in health, through richer or poorer until death do them part. I naively continued, not knowing I had been illegally married to many men. I had made those very same vows but the bed was my altar. In The Old Testament, the traditional marriage was arranged between a man and a girl's father. The man would ask to marry his virgin daughter; the date and time would be set. There was no two hour-long wedding, but there were maybe one or two witnesses. The father would hand the man a white purity cloth. The man would take the girl to a room, lay the purity cloth down and have sex with her. The girl would shed blood because she was a virgin, and the cloth was then handed to the father so he had proof that his daughter was indeed a virgin when they married. There was never a ceremony. Sex was what bonded a wife to her husband. This was her submission to him. To have sex with someone that is not your spouse is considered adultery. Sex taking place outside a marriage is breaking a covenant with God. My covenant with God had been broken because I was a broken person fostering sinful behaviors.

Often times I would ask God for deliverance, though I was never really ready to receive it, allowing the devil to come back ten times stronger when I closed the door on my deliverance. Sin felt too good to let go. But God still had His hands on me, offering blessings by sending spiritual people in my life that saw the best in me. When I saw only the worst. The enemy also wanted to bless me. He too would send people in my life to evoke the sin in me. I began questioning a lot of people in my life. It was in those moments of uncertainty that I realized I had attracted all these people because of where my heart was and where I was spiritually. I was filled with anger, fear, rejection, bitterness and pain, so spiritually I attracted broken people that had been battling with the very same demons I had been dealing with. And because I had soul ties with them, I was in bondage to them. My friends and the people I hung around were a reflection of what was inside of me. In due time, I realized it was time for me to let go of those friendships and the soul ties that bound me to sin. I was no longer able to relate to my friends because I began to live in my truth which made change possible. I asked God for a sound mind, and He came in and delivered me from living in my emotions. Emotions were only causing more havoc in my life. Having a sound mind allowed me to sit down and think things through. Living an emotionally charged life took away so many blessings that were promised to come my way. I was so wrapped up living life based on the impulses of my emotions doing things out of fear, anger and rejection. Now, before I do anything, I make sure my emotions are checked at the door. I make sure whatever I do comes from a place of love and in doing this, God has surrounded me with like people, people that are able to check their emotions and come from a place of love.

It was in those moments, God revealed to me that the people I had considered to be friends were not loyal to me. They were only loyal to their need for me and once their need was satisfied, so was their loyalty. Everyone with me was not for me. I had friends that would only call to gossip and I had to accept that those soul ties I had formed with them would no longer conform to the life Christ had planned for me. These soul ties had to be cut, but I was so afraid of losing friends. God would put it on my heart to respond to them in such a way that severed our friendship after a few phone calls. They would call and start to gossip and my response would be, "Well that's too bad. We are going to pray for her." The phone calls became less and less until God filtered out all the gossipers in my life. God did this in every aspect of my life. I was beginning to feel like I was stuck in a place of trying to figure out who I was and who I was becoming. I was losing all of my worldly friends. I had no one else to talk to but God. He removed everything draining to me, everything toxic, and poisonous to my faith.

I had been dating a guy. Everything on the outside seemed well put together. He was not like other men I had dated. He was not about the street life, held down a full time job as well as a part time job. I thought I knew him well enough. We spent a lot of time together, even talked about having a future together. I was still young in the world and trying to figure life out. He was a bit older than me, a bit more experienced in life, but the affection we had for one another was certain. We had a connection that could only be explained as love. For the first time in a long time, I had opened up a bit. I did not know much about his mother due to their distant relationship. We did not talk much about his past. Whenever the subject came up, I instantly knew he was trying to let his past be the past. That really did not bother me much because we all have chapters in our lives we are unable to read out loud. We never argued, fussed or ever had a fight for that matter. And just as the devil dressed him up, I respected this man. He was another hurt soul I thought I could fix. I never knew what he had built up inside of him waiting for the perfect time to be released. I saw this man every day and he never even so much as hurt a fly in front of me.

I remember explaining to him early on in our relationship that my son took a trip or two to California every year and stayed for the summer. Because we talked about everything, I explained in detail how close I was with the family of my son's father and that when I dropped him off, I would be visiting California for an entire week. I explained to him that I considered their family an extended part of my family. We had built a bond over the years and they were my family. I explained that I would be staying at my son's great grandmother's home. He was fine with all the details. I also advised him that my son's father would be probably stop by to spend time with our son from time to time. He was also fine with that. He knew the romantic relationship between my son's father and I was completely over.

Summer came and the plans were made for my son to go to Cali. Vacation time had been approved at my job. My son and I were all set. I remember telling him my son and I would be leaving soon. Everything was fine leading up to us leaving. We spent some time together the day before and that was that…until I got to California. I called him as soon as our plane landed to notify him we made it safely and I would call in a few hours after we settled in. Within the first few hours of our being in California, his insecurities began to show.

Overwhelmed by the "welcome, we missed you" greeting we received, a few hours passed. My phone rang. Looking at the caller id, I remembered I had completely forgotten to call and check on him. I quickly answered my phone. I guess he was not expecting many people or my son's father to be at my son's great grandmother's house because his tone suddenly changed. I do not remember much, but I remember us arguing about me not calling when I said I was and my son's father being there to see him. I became upset. I told him I was not going to argue with him especially while I was a guest in someone's home. He accused me of being with my son's father saying that is why I did not call him back. After the accusation was put out there, I hung up the phone, mystified. How could this man I had been with, the man that knew my situation with my son's father accuse me of cheating on him with my son's father of all people?

I knew hanging up the phone was not the right thing to do and would not bring me any positive gain, but I was shocked and confused by his accusations. I needed a moment to get my thoughts together. Maybe I did something wrong. Was I wrong for not calling him back when I told him I would? I instantly put the blame on myself but before I could pick up the phone to explain, he called me back. This time, he was much more aggressive. The language he used was foreign to me coming from him. I could not get more than two words in. By then, everyone noticed my happy demeanor had turned sour. Flustered and a bit rattled, I went into another room and my son followed. Shaking frantically, with my son's eyes boring into my heart, I hung up. The phone calls, text messages and voice mails followed one after another, minute after minute, hour after hour. I had no choice but to turn my phone off. It was too much for me. I told myself I would give him some time to come down from whatever he was on. Clearly, he was not himself and maybe it was the fact that he was use to having me around and could not deal with me being gone. Boy, was I wrong.

The next morning, things had settled down, at least for me. I still had my phone off. I received a call from my son's father on the house phone. He said he wanted to take my son and me to lunch as a thank you to me, and a token of his appreciation. I accepted. I did not see anything wrong with two parents sitting down for the first time in years and actually getting along for the sake of their child. I turned on my phone, bypassing the accumulated text messages and voice mails. I dialed his number. He was yelling and screaming at me before I ever had the opportunity to tell him my plans for the day. At this point, I was fed up, especially knowing I did nothing wrong. I ended it right then and there, but of course he called back and sent many apologetic text messages.

My time in Cali neared an end, but the start to my summer was right around the corner. The day of my flight, I awoke early to get a head start on packing my things for my return home. My son beat me up and lay in bed staring at me. Unfazed by this rare occurrence, I asked no questions. Even though it was highly unusual for my son to wake up before me, I just thought it was because I was leaving. We got up. I made breakfast for the two of us, and we spent some time together before it was time for me to leave. I kissed my son and gave him the biggest bear hug before leaving him with his grandmother to board the plane. My son had been to California many times and spent many summers there with his dad and family. As I was gathering my things, he cried out, "Please don't go!" I placed my things down to comfort him not knowing something was placed on his heart to say this to stop me from traveling back home. It was a Saturday morning and I already had my night planned. There was no getting out of my first night back home without my son. I glanced at my son one last time, tears still flowing from his eyes. In his four-year-old voice, he pleaded with me one last time. Unwilling to give in to his pleading, he told me to be careful. But the way he said it was like a father telling his only daughter, his only child to be careful. I asked my son why he wanted me to stay. All he could mumble was, "I'm worried about you." His eyes held genuine worry. I did not understand where this was coming from because he had never done this before. We traveled to California frequently, that was his home away from home. His reaction to me leaving was puzzling, but I never stopped to really question his behavior. I left my son as he cried in his grandmother's arms.

I boarded the plane with this on my heart. It was not the fact that my plane ticket had already been purchased because I could have paid the extra money to reschedule my flight. It was not the fact that my son had his grandmother there to comfort him. It was the fact that I failed to realize God was using my son to stop me from coming home because indulging in sin was more important to me. I was so committed to getting back to my sinful ways, that I would not listen when God himself was speaking to me.

It was Saturday evening and nightfall was fast approaching. The only thing I could think about was getting into character. This was a habitual activity that became a part of life for me for many years; getting dressed for a night filled with drinking and club hopping. My friends and I had a ritual before going to the club. We would hit a few blocks or drive around the club a few times with our windows down, music blasting, seeking the attention of many. This one particular night was no different from the rest. The first club we stopped at would be my last for that night although there were plans to go to a few others. We walked in, welcomed by loud music and a crowded dance floor. We circled the inside of the building a few times, just to let our presence be known and to see who of importance was in the building. Then, we made our way to the bar to order a few drinks even though we were still a bit tipsy from the drinks we chugged down prior to our arrival. Caught off guard, I was asked to dance. We made our way through the crowd to the dance floor. I shared a dance with a gentle stranger, but our two-step was unexpectedly interrupted by the person I had broken up with just days prior. Stunned to see him there, the first question out of my mouth was, "What are you doing here?" He asked if we could talk and if it was okay that he cut in on the dance. The gentle stranger asked if I was okay. I slowly nodded for his approval to cut in. I was not scared, but I was uncertain of his intentions as he requested that we go somewhere to talk. Still dancing, laughing and having a good time, I quickly turned down his request. He asked me once more, much sterner in his stance and much more inflexible in his tone as he took hold of my arm. My intoxicated one hundred and twenty pound body tried to swing my arm to get away from the strong hold he had on me. He asked me one last time, but as our eyes met there was a disturbing blackness that commanded his body. I was frightened and pleaded for him to let go of my arm.

Still intoxicated, I knew what was going on but I was unable to make sense of anything. By the time I knew it, he had pulled me out of the club with my arm still in his hand yanking me towards the street. The welcoming music had stopped in my head. Looking around at the faces outside the club, every face I looked at had this vague hesitant expression. Then, I heard a faint voice in the background advising him to let me go. My friend was coming to my aid. I stumbled trying to break free from his grip, but before I knew it, we were at his car. He opened the passenger door and pushed me. I fell in and he slammed the door behind him.

In the car, he kept repeating, "I just want to talk." It was like he was trying to convince himself, while something of a wicked nature flooded his thoughts. I was frightened. This was not the person I once knew. He now had a sinful stench reeking from his pores. By this time, the alcohol had completely left my system and I was fully conscious. I tried unlocking the door to get out the car, but he quickly locked the door. With a much more frantic motion, I tried getting out the car again. This was another failed attempt, as he quickly pulled off with my door still open. The force from him pulling off slammed my door and I heard the automatic locks once more. We drove around while I pleaded with him to take me back to my car. We stopped in front of the home of the woman he called his play mom. The house was darkened and there were no cars in the driveway. He looked at me and repeated, "I just want to talk." I refused and demanded he take me to my car. I pulled out my phone to call my friend and he grabbed my phone. I pleaded with him to let me call my friend. He spoke not a word.

I remember looking at him and him gazing over at me. At some point, the punches began. The first time he punched me, I screamed and grabbed my face, shocked. I was so frightened because a man had never hit me. I honestly think I was more surprised that the man that claimed he loved me was hitting me like I was another man. We stopped at a stoplight. I tried to open my door to get out. I had it in my mind that he was not going to let me go willingly. I got my door opened. The light was red. I was going to make a run for it, but he sped off almost causing an accident. Horns blared and tires screeched as other cars came to a halt. He gripped the back of my blouse and pulled me back into the car. Again, the door closed from the force of him speeding off. I had endured many punches to my face. There were no body shots just face punches and by this time, I knew I had to fight back. The only thing I could hear was my mother's voice telling me to fight. My face had become numb from his punches and because I could not feel anything, I decided to fight back. Something came over me that lifted me from the passenger's seat straight to his side of the car. I remember thinking that if I was going to die, so was he. He was still driving the car, uncontrollably. I was praying someone would notice and call the police. There was one final blow to my face, a blow that sent me falling back in my seat.

Then there was darkness, nothing but light from the stars gleaming down on me. I looked up at those stars and everything became still. I remember the smell of the summer's night air. It reminded me of the scent of my son's clothing. I stopped fighting. I stopped crying. My body became numb. A calmness came over me and in that moment, I was ready to die. I had it in my mind that I was going to die at that park and he was going to dump my body in the lake. He popped his trunk and I trembled from my head down to my feet with terror. I did not know what he was looking for, but whatever it was he was not able to find it. That is when more blows came to my face and then my body. The funny thing is, I was so ready to die. I could no longer feel the punches. I remember screaming, "Just kill me!" He replied in a calm humorous voice, "Now that would be too easy, wouldn't it?" I looked up to the sky and said, "And I left my son crying in his grandmother's arms." That was the only thing I could think about, how I left my son. He heard me and picked up my frail body from the ground, placing me back in his car. This went on for hours as I watched him drop my phone, my shoes and all of my belongings out his window. I knew he was going to kill me. He was driving around to find the perfect spot. He had already dumped any evidence that I was with him and now he was plotting to kill me and would see it through this time.

We were on a darkened street. I kept thinking that I would never see my son again, they would probably never find my body and he would get away with it. I decided to turn my back to him so he would be unable to see me lift the lock on the door. I was trying to be as still and as quiet as I possibly could so he would not suspect anything. I managed to unlock the door. I quickly opened the door and jumped out of the moving car with my body rolling against the hard, cold ground. I heard his car engine stop. I don't know how I managed to stop rolling, but I did. I jumped to my feet and ran. Soon, I heard the roar of his car following right behind me. I never looked back. I never stopped running. Something told me to start yelling for help. I listened to that voice as I heard his car go in the opposite direction. I did not know where I was. I had no money, no phone and I was barefoot.

And in that instant, my perspective about all men changed. I lost my trust. With all the drug dealers and thugs I dated, I never felt threatened by any of them. They never laid a hand on me. It wasn't until I stepped out of my comfort zone and dated someone that was the complete opposite of what I was use to dating. I thought my prayers had been answered. Here he was, what I thought to be, a God fearing man standing right in front of me. I was on a rampage with a vengeful seductive heart. Selfishly, I tried to hurt every man I was with after him. I made them pay for his mistakes, my grandfather's mistakes as well as my father's. I wanted to hurt men in every way I was hurting, but there would be many more of his type. I dated guys who were good guys until something triggered their pain. Years later, I asked God for forgiveness for hurting others out of my own hurt.

Just as God knew my heart, so did the devil. Relationship after relationship, the devil would dress the next man up, and the next man I encountered would be more cunning, more convincing than the one before. Too often, I was deceived by his persuasive talk on religion and his fanciful walk towards spirituality. Worldly men still living by their flesh disguised as religious men or spiritual men. The religious men went to church on Sunday, getting the word and leaving church still living by their flesh. Church was all that I required of men. Then there were the spiritual men who never went to church but could quote scriptures. These men said they were totally into God, walking in the will of God but still satisfied their flesh, indulging in illegal sexual activities.

Mentally exhausted from years of pursuing the same type of man, I could not understand why I continuously ran into the same types of men. At this time, I was in the beginning stages of my journey to faithfulness. God began to reveal the patterns of the ungodly to me for He knew the desires of my heart. All I desired was to have a religiously spiritual God fearing man. The devil picked up on this and would send me one or the other.

I would get so angry at God because of the men He allowed to hurt me. But He was only giving me what I sowed. Every man I ever dated was a reflection of me spiritually. I sowed lust and in return, that is what I received. How could I ask God for a good God fearing man, when I was not a God fearing woman? How could I tell God all the things I wanted in a man, when I had not yet filled the voids of my heart? What I failed to realize was all the things I said I needed in a man were things I needed to fulfill within my heart. I would ask God to send me someone that not only thought I was beautiful but told me I was beautiful. But I could not tell myself I was beautiful. I would ask God to send me someone that loved me for me, when I did not love the woman I was. I would ask God to send me someone that would cater to my every need when I was selfishly unwilling to cater to the needs of my mate. I was asking for things I was not ready for and because of my disobedience, God had to show me who I really was by allowing these men to enter into my life. Used as my reflection, He was showing me my heart mirroring back pieces of me I was unwilling to see.

I held on to that pain for many years until I learned I would not be able to release what I was unable to confront. I so badly wanted him to suffer. The judicial system failed me. And because he did not have a previous record and a "good job he did not want to lose" as he explained to the judge, he only received a few weekends in jail. He would live his life Monday through Friday, and then on Friday after 4 pm he had to check himself into jail and stay until Sunday. Forgiveness had to start with me because I blamed myself for that night. How could I have been so stupid to let it get that far? Why didn't I just leave when I noticed him there? I pondered these thoughts in my head. But to forgive means not to seek revenge. It meant to let go of the anger and bitterness I built up inside. This did not mean forgiving the incident or even denying it happened. It meant for me to renounce the anger so it would no longer affect my future relationships. I surrendered my hostile feelings to God. Remembering that forgiveness was for my benefit, letting go of that pain was the best thing I could have ever done.

Chapter Five

A Manipulated Love

Captivated by a charming man whom I had known for years. We had lost touch several years prior when he accepted a job working on the road. He was the type of man that exuded confidence and positive energy, exactly what I needed after a bad break-up. He was everything I lusted after - street cred turned business man. And because I was a lustful woman, my idea of a good man was entirely based on a realm of fantasies that seemed picture-perfect. Blinded by what I interpreted love to be, I really could not see him for who he was. I allowed myself to be caught up with desire. I saw in him only what lust permitted me to see. This behavior was repetitive for me. Lust was the only commonality between us. Another emotionally unstable man that lusted after a woman whom herself was emotionally unstable at that time. I became soul tied with him only seeking happiness. It took us no time to get back to how we were. He became my best friend. He was the first person I called whenever I had exciting or bad news. He called not wanting anything, but we would end up talking on the phone for hours about everything seeking advice from one another or just communicating about daily successes or struggles. And when he came home, we always made sure our time was spent catching up. There was never a need to have sex. We enjoyed having a good time in each other's company and this went on for months.

Then, I was introduced to the Jezebel spirit. Incomparable to the other spirits I had dealt with, this spirit was much more intelligent and cunning. I was not aware of the nature of the spirit. So when this spirit presented itself to me, I confused this spirit to be nothing more than a bit aggressive at times and somewhat controlling. The Jezebel spirit conceals its most pernicious actions behind the veil of control and manipulation. Most people, if they are not careful in their inquiry, confuse the Jezebel spirit with a spirit of sexual seduction as I did. Jezebel will use seduction to hold people captive in their emotions. Seduction does not have to come in the form of sex. It can come in the form of a subtle emotional bond.

The Jezebel spirit uses seduction to form a soul tie with someone in order to gain her control. Once the control has been established, Jezebel's seducing entanglement is used as emotional manipulation. The spirit of a Jezebel usually attaches to women in order to redirect the order of the home, seeking to neutralize male authority causing the male (Ahab) to doubt their own decisions including their manhood. In Satan's kingdom, the women rule and his only objective is to strip men of their authority. The companion spirit to Jezebel is the Ahab spirit. This is because it takes an Ahab spirit for Jezebel to be effective and operate unchallenged. The Ahab spirit prefers a male host, in which Jezebel will use the Ahab for domination stripping him of his leadership. Both spirits will need to be fueled by the other in order to accomplish their goals, as they use each other for their own benefit. The Ahab will use Jezebel to do most of his dirty work, while Jezebel will use Ahab to dominate under her false authority.

And although the Jezebel and I have probably battled against the same demons at one time or another, the spirit of a Jezebel's pain comes from deep-rooted rejection. With the presence of brokenness in her heart that constantly attempts to fill a love deficiency, Jezebel's pain is driven more by rebellious pride, manipulation and arrogance. Rebellion comes in different forms. Rebellion for the Jezebel spirit is a crafty love of power that takes cover behind her religious works. Everything is a reaction released from the flesh. The Jezebel abuses her authority in leadership positions mostly seen in her family as the boss. Jezebel is against natural male authority. She is a woman with issues deeply rooted in her heart in connection with male authority. Jezebel has been harmed and/or abused by a male authority figure of her past either conversely because her father abused her, spoiled her or he never confronted her mannerisms as a child. Slowly, the devil broke her down starting in childhood and built her back up as Jezebel herself over the years.

The Ahab son has an addled soul. As my faith began to ascend, my ex professed to me all the reasons why I could not grow in faith and why I would not ever be good enough for him. His fears reminded me of who I was in his eyes. In those moments, I knew I could not settle for anything less than my destiny, including him. I was stuck in something I knew was no longer part of my present or future. The fantasy level of open communication hindered our relationship. We only disclosed to one another what we thought the other should know. We hardly ever discussed our real feelings, and even though I was physically in the relationship, I was downright lonely mentally. Destruction awaited within the infatuation created between us. Together, we were religiously building our relationship on the strength of each other instead of the strength of Christ. The love of God was not present in our relationship. I was unable to see the objects of my lust so I began to idolize him, putting his needs and wants before mine. He came before God. And because he was on the road the majority of the time, distance determined our fate. At this time, it was easier for me to judge others and their relationship because I spent a lot of my time idolizing my ex from afar. Blind to my own relationship, I never knew what he was like up close. I became infuriated with God. Everyone I knew was either getting married, buying houses together or were in a good place in their relationship, and here I was living a counterfeit life with my ex on the inside. On the outside, however, we were the perfect couple. It just seemed like the more time I spent in the relationship, the faster to nowhere I found myself. Still, I followed his decisions with every career choice. Even though I disagreed with them at times. I did this in order to make our relationship work. I would sacrifice my needs, but in reality I was denying myself the opportunity to be heard. For years, I could not understand why it was so hard for him to figure out his role, why it was so hard for him to make decisions without consulting his mother. I felt like it was very hard for him to hear me, but he heard her loud and clear. I would try to advise him on certain things that were going on with us, as well as in his life, but my opinion never mattered. Only that of his mother's. I originally thought he was a momma's boy, so I brushed his ways to the side. But, the Ahab spirit would rise up again showing me many principles one should avoid. The principles he stood by were the perfect example of everything a man should not be. This type of spirit is the true symbolism of giving up authority and then abdicating his responsibilities to his girlfriend/wife because Ahab is emotionally unstable causing him to doubt his own abilities, which led to feelings of inadequacy and increased frustration. And because of this frustration, he refused to take spiritual headship for his family. He had been conditioned to rely on the Jezebel spirit.

From childhood, Jezebel emasculated her son. In adulthood, he needed a woman to take care of him and make the decisions. Ahab does not know how to operate in authority so he will also seek out a Jezebel girlfriend and will eventually desire to make her his wife. Bringing me around the Jezebel spirit was an unconscious attempt at grooming me to become a Jezebel; wanting me to learn in detail how to take authority over him because he had been groomed for so long he did not know how to take his own authority back from the

Jezebel spirit. I did not fall victim to this principality. Because Jezebel is a higher ranking spirit, she will have lower ranking spirits operating under her. This is what I was being groomed to become. This offering was placed before me a number of times. However, because I was already spiritually awakened, I declined. He went back to his mother's rule, and although he did not say it, he much rather preferred to be around his mother because he did not know how to be a man. He had to find someone to hand over his responsibilities and submit to because he did not know how to walk in the authority God placed upon him. I never allowed myself to become angry because I knew it was the spirit and not the woman. And because I knew in God's eyes it is not the role of a man to rely on a woman financially to ensure his stability. I knew Jezebel is self-glorifying and needs to rule. Most of the time, women with this spirit have no idea what is motivating or controlling them.

Jezebel always came through in his time of need handling all of his major responsibilities including his judicial dealings. Many times I wondered if it was all done for the sake of retaining control over him. Still, I remained submissive, allowing him to lead as I followed, being a good woman while trying to prove my loyalty to him but lingering within the walls of his heart were the works of the Ahab spirit. He had no clue his mother was operating under the Jezebel spirit. Sadly, he had no clue he was bred of the devil. I knew the natural order of the home was that the man is the head of the woman because demons will always seek to destroy the weaker of the gender first, which is a woman. Thus, man is the head of the home so he can seek God for strength. But when it came to making any decisions, he was the one to make the least amount of effort while all the difficult, pressing things were handed over to Jezebel and because Jezebel was the head of her home, Ahab was use to an aggressive woman not a submissive one. Because Jezebel refuses to submit to God, her actions are used to mock God's order. What comes from her heart is not true submission. It is false pretense. Jezebel fed me with spiritual pride to gain a soul tie, satisfying her need to control in order to feel secure. Jezebel is a master of manipulation as her overbearing personality encouraged sin putting up a good veil of treachery, speaking lies to her advantage for my compromise, using flattery saying what I wanted to hear to win me over. I quickly began to confide in her. She was tremendously subtle in her deception, but I also came to know Jezebel is extremely jealous of anyone they perceive to be a threat or anyone that gets close enough to influence someone already under their control.

I tried to avoid the same heartbreaking mistakes I witnessed my mother endure, but the choices I made in lust severely altered my thinking in my reality. I never really understood women that said they stayed for the children until I became one of those women. My body was still physically present in the relationship, but emotionally and mentally I had left a year prior. I was completely depleted from being emotionally ignored. He showed me in his actions and by the odious words that rolled off his tongue that I was unworthy of being noticed. I spent several unhappy years with a man that did not see me for who I really was. He was unable to explore me outside his comfort zone, outside the reigns of the Jezebel's control. Our relationship became repulsive. I could no longer stay with someone that did not see an issue with their actions. Everything he did was justified by the lack of value he had for me. Misery loved company, and I wallowed in his dolor, allowing him to entertain his own plight. I was his consolation prize. I lost a piece of myself in that relationship. Not asking for what I wanted or needed, I only accepted what was available from him. I gave up on who I was just to be with him, while he pacified me with promises he knew he was unable to keep. Operating in pride because he was uncertain of who he was as a man, resisting correction because pride acted as an insecurity in his identity, he became frustrated allowing his insecurities to flow out onto me. A crowd seeker, he was nothing alone, falsely manipulating people, portraying himself as such a great guy.

Fighting with his own demons, he was incapable of telling me how beautiful I was because of the ugliness that was deep seeded within him. He always had a problem with the way I looked and dressed. He was self-conscious in his appearance, so he constantly put me down to boost his ego. This is why I never changed, not even with the smart comments. I knew it had nothing to do with me because I always kept myself up, even on my worst days. It had everything to do with him and his self-perception. He tried to destroy my self-confidence because he had very little of his own. Slowly, I began to give this man all my power until I was powerless. I relied on him for my every waking need. I imagined the ideal man he should have been and expected him to live up to it. I was too caught up in who he was not and too caught up in fixing my father.

It actually took me losing myself to find my strength in this relationship. I was so drained from all the malice, I often cried myself to sleep at night probing for answers as to why he did not understand me and why I was so uncomfortable with the way he was treating me. Truth be told, he did not know how to make me happy because he looked at me through the eyes of the spirits that were attached to him. All that was in him, was what brought him to me to begin with. I constantly had to prove myself to this man while being ridiculed for not being a ride or die chick. But in my mind, I knew a ride or die chick didn't mean being a fool. It meant being responsible enough to know that I had children that I had to be home for to make their breakfast and do their laundry. And I wouldn't be able to do that if we were both locked up or dead. Judging from his actions, he thought he would affect me in some way. My silence was erroneously mistaken as a weakness. I was in his shadow and when he looked at me as a responsibility instead of his helpmate, I knew. I was not happy in the relationship and neither was he. When an individual's season is nearing an end in your life, God begins to reveal their pattern. And, as they begin to reveal themselves, God will allow you to see all their bad qualities. I needed someone to talk to, someone who could relate to me other than my friends. I was in search of an unbiased opinion from someone that knew him like the back of their hand. It was then that I realized I was in the reigns of the Jezebel spirit because I had been going to her seeking advice on what I should do. Unable to recognize her subtle works and hidden, impure motives, I followed her teachings. She used information I gave as leverage and would only share tidbits of information with me regarding her son. The spirit of Jezebel operating in his family had a very intense stronghold. There were never any boundaries when he dealt with Jezebel. He was passive and very submissive to her ways. The spirit at first acted very silently. I was now in a stage of my life where I realized I was praying the wrong prayer against this spirit, constantly praying to rebuke its controlling nature. But dealing with this type of spirit, prayer alone is not enough. The Jezebel spirit will do and say things and then find some way to rationalize it, thinking their behavior is perfectly justifiable. Blindly following the leading of this spirit, his mother was deeply entrenched with the spirit playing the good cop-bad cop game. The spirit knew scripture well. I was very impressed. This spirit is also good with playing mind games. Often times, I felt disoriented. The chaos brought much disorder. Where there is a Jezebel spirit, there is an Ahab spirit not too far away. With strong dominance and control of her home, she demands loyalty, is extremely authoritative and easily offended when her authority is questioned. Control and manipulation are the two strongest qualities, but she also has a lust for power. The Jezebel is more spiritual than the spirit of Ahab. She takes the leading role using her Ahab's emotional stresses.

I never really knew the face of truth dealing with a man who was insecure and had his ego to protect him. I was dealing with a man who did not see me as his equal; he did not view me as his helpmate. Although he would say he did, my heart knew otherwise. There were countless situations that proved I did not have a voice and there came a time when I knew everything between us was finished.

That was my new beginning. So I humbly left and I haven't looked back since. The best revenge for me was watching him decay in his negative energy. Now he is the one drowning in all my accomplishments while I'm staying afloat. And without delay, I was left with an oenomel, of something combining strength and sweetness — the taste of victory. I was not afraid of walking away. I was afraid of walking away and becoming everything he secretly thought I was not going to be. He did not deserve to know the real me, so I left him to criticize the person he thought I was. For all that it was and everything it wasn't, I could not stomach another failed relationship, but I will never run back to what broke me. It took me a while to mend the shattered pieces from this relationship. Now, I am at peace, mended and whole.

While God commanded us to forgive, He never told us to continue trusting those that violate our trust. Mustering up the strength, forgiveness for me was rendering to God the right to take care of justice. I had to learn how to stop trying to be in control of the situation and just *let go and let God*. I learned in the act of refusing to transfer the right to exact punishment, I was showing God that I did not trust Him. I learned that forgiveness is a process just like love is a process and it would take some time to work through my emotional healing. Until I was able to control my emotions, I would not be blessed. Forgiveness taught me how to respond in such a way that I would not expect people to be any different than who they truly are. Too often my quiet nature was misconstrued as being weak and I thought that if I forgave them, I would indeed be what they portrayed me, weak. But I learned that forgiveness is not about being weak because it takes less energy to forgive than it does to stay mad. I realized the more I was able to release myself from the bitterness, the more I was able to see God.

Chapter Six

The Point of Defeat

Remembering my defeats and losses at the hand of the devil and never remembering my successes and victories in Christ, I became a rope in a spiritual tug of war. The devil had it on my soul that my life was infinitely flawed and I had no purpose. I began to doubt everything I had accomplished. In our adversity, the devil can take many forms, often times in the things that are wished for. But my case was much different because God had already blessed me with the desires of my heart and I had already begun my journey in the walk towards faithfulness leading to the path of obedience. Reluctant to willfully fall back in sin, the devil sent his demons to attack me in any way they could. And because the devil had already known it would be impractical to get me to physically engage in the act of sin, he came for me mentally.

Having to always be the strong one and always pushing myself toward greatness, I was the one who always got things done and the one everyone knew they could depend on. I was also the person that took on responsibilities from people that God never intended me to take. Too often defined as stoic, "The Strong Black Woman," capable of holding down my own. I was a single mother of two that always did what needed to be done. Life for me at all times was always interrupted by the needs and wants of my children. I worked hard, saved what I could, and eventually obtained my college degree. With all the hard work I put into school, it finally paid off. A few months later, I landed a position at my current employer making a salary one could only fathom. A few months after that, my children and I moved into our dream home. My life, two years prior, consisted of a position that was leading to a dead end and late night studying for a major test in one class while trying to complete homework for other classes with only two hours of sleep before I had to get up and get myself and the kids ready for school and work. Anyone looking in from the outside would say I had the perfect life, deceived by my pleasant demeanor and my spirit of empowerment. I was well put together. No one would ever see me as anything less, but everything you were unable to see about me was a complete and utter mess. No one knew of or saw the demons I fought every day.

I had accomplished so much, but I had also become overwhelmed, stressed and exhausted from trying to be supermom. I had so much on my plate. I searched for a home to purchase for over a year. I had just graduated and obtained my bachelor's degree with no breaks in between semesters, and the new position I accepted was nothing I perceived it to be. The job was so stressful and overwhelming. I had welcomed anxiety. I experienced anywhere from one to three anxiety attacks a day. I do not know why I had it in my mind that making the kind of money I was making, the new position would be easy. I was so stressed out my hair was not only breaking off but coming out. God tested me with this position. This position was one of the most challenging jobs I have ever had, but I was determined not to give up. I had been on my grind for the last three years, never stopping to enjoy life, too afraid that if I took a break, I would lose my drive; my passion to succeed. I was determined to finish what I started because I had already accomplished so much. I was striving for success, but I honestly did not know whom I was doing it for. I was cheerless in my success. I could not let all of what had been accomplished slip away. Then one day, I was unable to be perfect, unable to hide behind what everyone perceived me to be. I was the "strong black woman" who hid a thousand feelings behind the smile of divinity. Maintaining a smile when co-workers, friends and family came around even though my mind was being defeated. And even though I had all this good surrounding me, I was unable to see it, unable to enjoy it. My exterior image was a contradiction with what was in the depths of my heart. I was giving up. The devil was winning the battle over my emotional health. I was mentally and physically drained. The depression and anxiety slowly took over my life. Not only was I waking up in the morning fighting the same demons I had been fighting with through the night, I went to work fighting through stress and forcing myself to get through the anxiety. I promised myself months before that I would not allow myself to have a victim mentality. I no longer had to blame others for my misfortunes. I no longer needed rescuing from my past. I no longer needed validation because I would be strong enough to fight through all my battles but I was too afraid to talk about it, too afraid to even speak the word. I was afraid that if anyone knew, I would no longer be the strong woman everyone knew me to be. I could not risk saying, "Hey, I am overwhelmed with these kids and need some help." I could not risk saying, "Hey, I am a bit stressed from work and could use a break." I could not risk telling my truth because that meant being vulnerable. I thought if I said something everyone would know and I would be judged and ridiculed. I thought everyone would think I was weak because for some odd reason when people think of anxiety and depression the first thought that comes to mind is a person who is completely unable to function, slowly wasting away, slowing disconnecting themselves from the world. And, because society says weakness in a black woman is intolerable, my mental health was rarely discussed with anyone.

The reality is mental health is taboo in the black community and too often stigmatized. Because the word "strong" is used to nominalize black women, I forced myself to suffer in silence. I could not acknowledge my mental turmoil because of the shame and embarrassment I thought would come with it. I held on to the legacy that I could carry the burden and weight of the world on my shoulders because black women are raised not to show their feelings. We are raised to not discuss whatever we are going through. We are taught through the actions of our mothers to just keep pushing and whatever you are feeling will pass. Because this is what we have seen our mothers do, it is something that does not have to be spoken. We learn it because we see it.

While some days were better than others, there were days I could not move from my bed. My sleep was riddled with insomnia, plagued by an overwhelming sense of failure and hopelessness. I fretted over everything, and then cared about nothing. My mental health was under attack. I realized I was living with high functioning anxiety, which permitted me to still live my everyday life with some sense of normalcy. But, I struggled with disquietude. I also realized high functioning anxiety was something I had lived with most of my life, never quite identifying it until my anxiety began to erode my perfectionism and over-achievement. My anxiety had a huge effect on my mental state at night. I was unable to fall asleep because I internalized my anxiety during the day, and by night it leaked out in the form of sleep disturbance. No matter how hard I tried, I was unable to relax, unable to sit still and unwind. With every passing day, it honestly felt like I could not breathe. Instead of grasping for air, I was grasping for life. And because I kept my anxiety buried, people had a very hard time understanding how I felt.

With my mind racing overtime all night, my face became unrecognizable. My reflection in the mirror told the visible signs of sleep deprivation. The mirror held all my secrets and intensified my every flaw. Probing for relief, I began to inquire about over the counter sleep aids. The first night I took one it appeared to work. One night turned into a custom I was unwilling to give up. I had been cajoled, lured in with a sound mind. However, still being moderately uneducated in the counsel of obedience, I frequently dabbled in idolatry serving two Gods, Christian by day and sinner by night. I had established myself in a nightly routine, referencing other sources. Rather than picking up my bible and relying on the word, I picked up my phone and relied on my daily horoscope seeking to find quick resolutions for what was taking place in my life. The door to my soul was now wide open. Never speculating this was part of his plan the devil had meticulously plotted against me. He initiated my insomnia, studied my sleep habits, became skilled in my routine, and then acted swiftly on my weakness. Now, he could finally have his way with me.

The devil works best at night and since I would not surrender to his ways during the day, he would come lurking for me at night after my nightly routine. First, the sleep aid as my body became weightless and easily attainable. Then, my horoscope described as a form of divination that was forbidden in the Bible. Fast asleep, I would occasionally wake up with night sweats. My gown would be soaked in sweat as if I had been submerged in uncomfortable temperatures for an extended period of time. Puzzled by what could have been a dream but seemed so real, every night I was involuntarily welcomed back to the devil's home, known to me as sin. I was no more of this physical world but of a world no saved Christian had ever seen before. I was drained from all the destruction the Jezebel spirit brought. At my wits end with my dealings with the Ahab spirit, I had been battling with temptations that looked like people I trusted but came in forms of adulteresses. I was honestly dealing with a few individuals who were attached to the spirit of a demon. I know this now because I have learned how ungodly spirits work. These spirits are strategic in their thinking. They will latch on to individuals that really care about you. These spirits are able to rise at their own will in individuals. A spirit is able to attach itself because that person is battling something that has them in bondage but will try to get you off track and pull you back into sin. There are some Christians out there who attend church every Sunday, sit in the front pew and can still be in their flesh and not know it. And then these Christians try to come preach the word to you with the enemy speaking through them. Since I was on my journey to being obedient, I knew all the temptation was nothing but the devil coming after me. For temptation was the only way he knew he could lure me, but I knew the cost of sin would subsequently result in death. I felt everything all at once attracted to me and began to work on my mind. This spirit's only objective was to try and make me as mentally unstable as it possibly could. But in my times of battle, I became the person that rescued me as a child. I became my mother. It was her strength that whispered confidence in my heart.

Black women are looked at as strong survivors. For so many years, I had been told, "You will get through this," "Tiff, you are strong," or "You will be okay." And me being the strong independent person I am, I internalized those emotions instead of dealing with them. I constantly told myself I would be okay but I really wasn't. I heard it so much I tricked myself into believing I was actually okay. My perception of what okay was, was an erroneous mask. I was also dealing with the spirit of fear. I was doing really well in life, and all of a sudden, I had this strong sense of fear come upon me. The force was so strong, I panicked and that is when all the doubt came into play. I feared I would lose my job. Then I would lose my house. And, what would happen to my children and me? Where would we go? I feared not having enough money to feed my children. Although I knew in my mind God would never allow any of this to happen as long as I trusted Him. He would be my provider. I still could not control this fear.

I was in mental warfare with many spirits that attached themselves to me because of the pain that I allowed to become deep rooted in my heart. But I was also in a battle with a much stronger more intelligent spirit that attached itself through a past soul tie I had not quite let go of, Jezebel. I was unable to find peace in whatever I did. It was there. I battled with it in my sleep. I was unable to rest and whenever I was able to close my eyes, I was quickly awakened by worry.

Constantly trying to be in control of my life, I spent many days asking God to bless my plans out of desperation and not out of faith. I was so weary and tired of trying that I never asked God what His plans were for me. I prayed for guidance, this time I was sure of wanting my deliverance. I laid all my sins at the altar and asked God to take over. I surrendered. I came to terms with my oppression. I was able to put all of my faith and trust in God, and in return He was able to give me the things it took for me to overcome my weaknesses. He provided me with instructions from the Bible and showed me favor as I read His word.

When I moved into my house, I did not realize God's plan. He put me in complete isolation to hear only His voice with no other distractions. He separated me from the things of my past because He knew I would allow them to follow me into the present. There were some Christian friends I had still living by their flesh. I took some time off from dating, some time away from friends. For the first time in decades, I was not attached to anyone. I had broken all ungodly soul ties and came to know God. I did the only thing I knew how to do. I put one foot in front of the other and trusted in God's plans. I began to put my faith in God instead of men, friendships, or people for that matter. He isolated me to start working on my heart. He changed my thought process by renewing my spirit which enabled me to see with a clean clear heart, enabling me to think with a clear clean mind allowing me to check my emotions and act out of love instead of bitterness, fear and pain.

And then there was stillness. My heart was at peace. I was finally delivered. God allowed me to see things as they were. By taking time out to know me, I began to understand who I was as a woman. I love the person I have become because I had to fight to become her. Today, I am who I am because of what I fought for. My greatest achievement was learning how to love myself.

At certain points in my journey, I reached new levels and at each level there were new demons. Sometimes when things were falling apart, they were actually falling into place. God fought my battles and made sure to arrange things in my favor. I began to understand how I contributed to my own pain by not asking for what I wanted so I stopped accepting whatever came along. I never had any clear, well-defined boundaries with anyone, which led to a lot of people encroaching upon my life. And because I was a person that put others before myself, I allowed many people to become thieves. These people unconsciously robbed me of my clarity because my clarity of self was based on other people's responses. Regrettably, how I treated myself was how I was treating God, putting myself last as I continuously put people and other things before Him. Learning in the process, being comfortable with the decisions I make now come from a place of love and peace and in the best interest of me and not the best interest of others. At some point in my life, I lost my integrity trying to please everyone. I am now at the place in my journey where I am at ease with knowing not everyone will agree with or understand the decisions I make. In the past, I always searched for other people's confirmation in my decisions. Now, I don't really care who agrees with what as long as I know it is for the best interest of "self."

I had people in my life that were not part of my destiny holding me back. I realized I had to completely separate myself from anything that was not a promise from God. Truthfully, all change felt like a complete and total loss at the time. I would hurt over walking away from toxic friendships and loved ones. But God's love would not allow me to walk in regret very long. The Lord would instruct me in specific detail on how to move forward. At times I was fearful of His destiny, often questioning His plans because I had not allowed God to be in control of my life for so long. God would not reveal all the details of my life to me because He knew I was not at a stage in my life where I could handle the details of my destiny. He knew I would not understand and return to being disobedient.

People created their own storms and got mad at me when it rained. These same people took notice of the change in my attitude towards them but failed to notice their behavior that made me change to begin with. I failed to see people for who they really were but in the same breath, I expected people to be how I saw them. I made a decision to see as it was, that way I would not have these expectations no one could ever live up to. If I had no expectations, then no one would ever have an opportunity to hurt me.

I had to also learn that love is not something you show, but something you feel and because you feel it, love will then be expressed through the actions of your heart. Learning this taught me that love is not supposed to hurt and if it does, it is something other than love. It is fear, attachment, idolatry, addiction or even possessiveness. No one's hurt aches out of love. I thought I loved so many people just to be fooled by the spirit of fear. Growing up, I was taught to be loved was simply to be wanted. It was hard to be responsive to love when my heart was overturned by the desire of sin. Love is so much bigger to me now. My perception is to love as God loves me. To me, loving someone means for their happiness to be the same as my happiness and nothing less.

I wandered around for many years thinking God owed me something, expecting men to be faithful to me when they were not faithful to God. I expected these men to submit to me when they were not submitted to God. I expected them to commit to me when they were foolishly uncommitted to God. I was expecting things from men I, myself, was not quite giving God. I was envious of those that were in a season of reaping, while sowing seeds of offerings that had nothing to do with the act of love and everything to do with performance with conditional gain.

God allowed me to go through a five-year period in life where I had to become transparent about what was meaningful to me in my purpose. I had no clue who I was. I had no identity. The self-image I created of who I thought I was, was a distorted mask. I lived day to day without a vision and as smart as I was with my degrees, it was difficult living an unfulfilled life because I could not live my life beyond the eyes of my own bitterness. There was no spiritual progression. And there he was, mischievously hidden behind all of my accomplishments. The devil placed it on my heart that in order for me to live life happily, I had to fulfill my worth by my accomplishments. I was vexed because the feeling that came with achieving was supposed to ultimately defeat the lingering void of rejection.

In the end, forgiveness had to start with forgiving myself. I had to forgive myself for all those that I hurt both intentionally and unintentionally.

Chapter Seven

Disguised Blessings

As individuals we get so wrapped up and consumed by what we do not have, we fail to realize the blessings that have been placed before us. For God so loved the world, His love manifested through His only begotten son. God loved me enough to provide me with four fathers. Still, I looked past my uncles, searching for my father's love.

God allowed me to see through my struggles that He was my provider and whatever my heart desired, He would provide. God was watching me closely. There was a time I became so frustrated at God. I had accomplished all this stuff. After that, nothing exciting ever happened to me. I was stuck in an unhappy and unexciting place. A few years passed, I was doing the right thing but not seeing any progress. I was going to work, taking care of my children and coming home, but my life just seemed like I was stuck once again. I knew I had more in me, but I honestly could not understand why I was not progressing. After all I had accomplished, I was back to being immovable. Nothing new was happening and I was becoming more and more frustrated by the day. God was testing my faith. I was honoring God but there was no proliferation. To be honest, it kind of felt like I was going in circles. I was absent in life once again, numb to the world, work, home and this book, the story of my life. But something was happening, something I could not see. My character was being developed. My spirituality was becoming stronger. I was being prepared for where God was taking me. And in those moments, I was also breaking every inherited psychological curse ever bestowed upon me and my family.

I was the first to ever leave the nest and go to college. I was the first in my family to obtain multiple degrees. I was the first straight out of college and unassisted to make the amount of money I made. I was the first in my family to purchase a home without the help of a spouse. I am the first in my family to press past her fears to step out on a limb and conquer fears and pursue something that was placed on her heart to do. I am the first one to break the persistent irrational fear that writing a book is something I could never do. I have broken every generational curse leading up to this point. And as long as I stayed chained to my history, my family and the coming generations would be fruitless and unfulfilled in their destiny. I received a vision and revelation in God's words. Because a new image of myself was emerging, people tried to talk me out of what God had already placed on my heart. But my heart was already moving towards what I kept in front of me. For I knew whatever God put on my heart, He was going to use for the betterment of self. Anything else was temporary and subject to change.

God tested me through the disappointments, the frustration, even through the betrayals. They were all put before me as part of God's plan for the building of my character and the breaking of generational curses. I would not become all I was created to be without first being mundane. I now know my purpose. I was created to subdue my family's curse. I was created to open the doors to my children's purpose. I was created to break the irrational fears that once subjugated our family's legacy. I was created to introduce my family to things they thought they would never be able to see or do. I realized I was waking something up in my mom and youngest uncle, something that had been buried away because of the faint voice of persistent irrational fears that told them they couldn't. My anointing superseded going to work with a smile on my face to a job I absolutely disliked, because I learned how to do the right things with the right attitude. My anointing superseded my boring life because I was being prepared and when God saw He could trust me in my boring, ordinary life, I passed the test, taking me into my extraordinary life, breaking the walls that once lead to a genetic predisposed curse.

I had to pass the test of faithfulness. I had to be faithful where God currently had me positioned. I had to prove that even in my most average, ordinary and boring days, I could still be my very best. I had to prove to God that even though I was unable to make any sense of the whys, I could still be faithful in uncertainty. I was taught the true definition of patience and in my patience I started to grow, showing God that I trusted Him. Even though I could not see the changes on the outside, I felt the changes on the inside. I was changing mentally and spiritually, being faithful right in the position I was in. God kept me hidden for He knew people would try to talk me out of my destiny. He knew I would probably talk my own self out of my destiny listening to them. God silenced me so I could hear only His instructions. He knew I would share His instructions for me to the wrong people and with their consolation, I would walk right out of God's will because they would not understand the conversations between me and God. I was hidden in a way that prevented outside interference.

I realized I did not need the love and confirmation of my grandfather or my father because I already had all the love and confirmation I needed from my uncles. Instead of having one father, God blessed me with four fathers who never had any expectations of me other than to be what I was destined to be. My uncles are a true representation of God's commitment to get love to me, for God knew how to give it to me in another way other than my father and grandfather. He gave it to me through my uncles. God did not give me the people I wanted, He gave me the people I needed.

The day of my graduation from college, I was so down because I had spent the entire night before cursing my father and granddad for missing yet another one of my huge accomplishments, the first in the family to graduate college. Graduation day came and I remember walking across the stage and being overwhelmed by joy as I looked in the audience and saw my uncles watching their 'only daughter' walk across the stage. In that moment, I realized my uncles had not missed one of my graduations and had been at my graduation for my associate's degree as well as my high school graduation. My uncles were there for the births of my children, every birthday I had, every mistake that was made. All this time I spent mad at the world for my father and grandfather not being in my life, God provided me with four great dads in one father's absence. All this time I spent searching I finally realized my father lived through each one of my uncles.

Uncle David, thank you so much for showing me tough love and teaching me how to speak up and stand up for who I am and what I believe in. Thank you for keeping me in line. I may have walked down a few dark paths, but you were always there to help me embrace my own path and see the truth. Thank you for loving me wholeheartedly even though at times it was evident you did not agree with every decision I made. Thank you for teaching me to always consider the facts. Thank you for teaching me to never accept anything at face value. Everyone has an agenda. Thank you for teaching me about boundaries and respect. Thank you for always telling me the truth and not just something I wanted to hear.

Uncle Anthony, the gentle soul, thank you for your patience with me and allowing me to be who I was as uniquely as I was. Thank you for teaching me not to judge a book by its cover. You taught me not to be impressed with people trying to impress. You are who you are and you have this glow about you that you don't need to impress. Thank you for letting me be me. Thank you for letting me get away with pure destruction from sun up to sun down and never laying a hand on me. Thank you for allowing me to ask you a million questions and never just saying because I said so or because that is just the way it is. Thank you for answering the strangest questions I had, even if you had to make something up.

Uncle James, thank you for teaching me the meaning of respect. You have always had this authority about you where you demanded respect be given. I learned by watching you that if you work hard, you will get the things you want. Thank you for teaching me that my word was all I had, so it better be good. I was too afraid of you to lie to you, but being afraid also taught me honesty is the best policy.

Uncle Billy, the debater, thank you for showing me to never back down in what I believed in even though I may have to debate to make a point. Thank you for encouraging my dreams. You never had anything bad to say about everything I have ever laid before you in terms of my future. You are always supportive, eager and intrigued with what's to come or what's next.

And to D. Pace, even though I am not biologically yours, you have always been in my corner since I was two years old. I know I haven't always said how much I appreciated what you do for me, so I am saying it now. Thank you. I am truly blessed to have experienced a love like yours. It is beyond comparison. And for this, I am forever grateful.

Collectively, my uncles taught me by showing me that you can tell a lot about a person's character based on how they respect their loved ones and elders. Thank you for opening every door for every elder that crossed your path and thank you for showing respect. Thank you all for being my biggest supporters. Thank you guys for not being perfect and being yourselves. You all taught me that perfection is a myth.

To my beautiful mother, thank you for giving me the foundation I needed. When Jesus said, "You are the salt of the earth," he said that to the likes of the believing mother. Mom, you are the salt of my life and I thank you for the wealth of discipline and love you gave me. Thank you for being yourself. In being you, you allowed me to better understand who I was as a woman and as a mother. Because of the loving bond we shared over the years, it led to the healthy, loving relationship that my daughter and I will always have. The most important attribute you hold is understanding. Thank you for not only showing me, but teaching me how to be a woman through your self-love and acceptance. With no days off, you have always been supportive, patient and consistent. Thank you for always believing in me and standing behind me with every decision I ever made. Thank you for helping me through every storm that has come and your many sacrifices. Thank you for your continuous trust in the Lord. Because of this you were able to be a great spiritual guide to me. You have played the role of counselor many times. For this, I love you.

And to my radiant Aunt Ann and phenomenal grandmother Beatrice, thank you for teaching me to never take anyone or anything for granted. Thank you both for teaching me the true definition of independence, standing on your own and persevering during difficult times.

Those who sow in tears will reap with songs of joy.

He who goes out weeping carrying seed to sow will return with songs of joy carrying

sheaves with him (Psalm 126:5-6).

These two verses unravel a very powerful message. In my times of doubt, I use the book of Psalm as a celebration of God's laws and wisdom. When I am lost, this book provides me with an enduring feeling of trust, hope and confidence in the Lord. The book of Psalm uses poetic devices and metaphors as encouragement so we as believers can use those tools in the present when we are faced with hardships.

The book of Psalm covers timeless traditions, which are as relevant today as when the hymns were written thousands of years ago. The scripture above comes from Deuteronomy, meaning "second law." Book five reiterates the covenant between God and his people, endowed to us to use as protection. In it, God tells us that obeying Him brings blessings to us. These verses teach us that there will be no spiritual harvest without tearful cultivation and we must trust in the Lord, rejoicing in His name. Sowing takes patience. Sowing takes hope and in due season, we shall reap what we sow. We sow in faith. We sow in obedience, and we sow in repentance. Sowing tears does not mean that our tears are what we plant. Sowing in tears refers to the shedding of tears during planting, planting with love for what we grow in faith. And as for what we reap, we will reap what we sow. If you sow faith, you will reap faith. If you sow love, you will reap love and if you sow with trust, you will reap trust.

In this Psalm, sowing is simply the work that has to be done even when there are things in our lives that make us weep. Crops will not wait until we are done solving our problems. If we want to eat in the future, we must go out and sow seed in the present whether we feel like it or not. This psalm teaches us the truth that there is still work that has to be done whether we are emotionally up for it or not. When there are jobs that need to be completed and you are full of tears, press on to do the job (cleaning the house, going to church, going to work, etc.) with tears because if you plant precious seeds with tears of love, you will reap precious fruit, blessings of joy.

I dedicate this book to:

Donte'Vion, Nevaeh, Uleta, Beatrice, Ann

David, Anthony, James, and Billy

www.ingramcontent.com/pod-product-compliance
Lightning Source LLC
Chambersburg PA
CBHW052207090426
42741CB00010B/2449